Essentials of Our Faith

What Christians Believe

by JoAnne Sekowsky

BASIC BIBLE STUDY SERIES

Aglow® Publications
A Ministry of Women's Aglow Fellowship, Int'l.
P.O. Box I
Lynnwood, WA 98046-1558
USA

AGLOW BIBLE STUDIES AND WORKBOOKS

Basic Series

God's Daughter
*Practical Aspects of a Christian
Woman's Life*

God's Answer to Overeating
A Study of Scriptural Attitudes

The Call of Jesus
Lessons in Becoming His Disciple

Christ in You
A Study of the Book of Colossians

Triumph Through Temptation
How to Conquer Satan's Lies

Keys to Contentment
A Study of Philippians

Drawing Closer to God
A Study of Ruth

Proving Yourself
A Study of James

Living by Faith
A Study of Romans

The Holy Spirit and His Gifts
A Study of the Scriptural Gifts

Kingdom Living
A Study of New Life in Christ

Coming Alive in the Spirit
The Spirit-Led Life

The Quickening Flame
A Scriptural Study of Revival

A New Commandment
Loving As Jesus Loved

God's Character
A Study of His Attributes

Essentials of Our Faith
What Christians Believe

Encourager Series

Restored Value
A Woman's Status in Christ

Invitation to a Party
God's Incredible Hospitality

Enrichment Series

Wholeness From God
*Patterns and Promises for Health
and Healing*

Teach Us to Pray
*'A Study of the Scriptural Principles
of Prayer*

The Holy Spirit
His Person and Purposes

The Word
God's Manual for Maturity

More Than Conquerors
The Christian's Spiritual Authority

The Beatitudes
Expressing the Character of Jesus

With Christ in Heavenly Realms
A Study of Ephesians

Workbook Series

Introduction to Praise
*A New Look at the Old Discipline
of Praise*

Time
Making It Work for You

How to Study the Bible
Eight Ways to Better Learn God's Word

Spiritual Warfare
Strategy for Winning

Defense Against Depression
The Way to Wholeness

Guidance
Knowing the Will of God

Write for a free catalog.

Table of Contents

Cover design by Ray Braun

Unless otherwise noted, all Scripture quotations in this publication are from the Holy Bible, New International Version. Copyright © 1973, 1978, 1984, International Bible Society. Other versions are abbreviated as follows: KJV (King James Version), TAB (The Amplified Bible).

ISBN 0-932305-37-7

Introduction

Who needs to study a book on the essentials of Christianity?

As I write this study, I see an audience that is at least fivefold.

First is the person I call the interested bystander or curious spectator. He is the person whose appetite has been sufficiently whetted to make him willing to listen to what we have to say. For you I can only pray that the Holy Spirit will kindle the facts of this study and set your heart on fire with the truths it contains.

Second, there is the non-Christian who is ready to seriously investigate the claims of Christianity. For you my prayer is that God will bless your searching and satisfy the longing of your heart for a deeper reality.

Third, this study is written for the new Christian. He is someone who has already accepted Jesus but knows very little about this new faith that he has embraced. For you I pray that God will give you the same excitement for His truths that He has placed in my own heart.

Fourth, this is a book for people, who because of early sporadic and piecemeal training, have never had a complete picture of what their Christianity is all about. For you I pray that the fuller picture of what God has done for us will enrich your life and fill you with gratitude.

Finally, this study is for those who want a simple review of these teachings. The things of God are always exciting. As you go over this familiar material, I trust that you will see fresh aspects of God.

For all of you I pray God's blessing as you study.

JoAnne Sekowsky

God the Father

Introduction

Who is God? Is He a benign old man with a long beard and thundering voice? Is He a judge who long ago made a set of rules and sits waiting eagerly for us to break one of them so He can punish us? Or is He a loving Father who wants only the best for His creation?

Discussion Question: Write a short paragraph describing your ideas about God. If you are in a group, share your description with the other members.

_____

_____

_____

All of us have an inadequate and often confused picture of God. In this first lesson, we want to clear up any misconceptions we may have about Him and give us a picture of who He really is.

Prayer

Lord God, please teach me to see You as You really are. Thank You.

Bible Study

Because we are physical beings with very finite (limited) minds, it is difficult for us to understand God.

Read **2 Corinthians 13:14.**
1. List the three persons named here.

_____

_____

Although He is one God, He also is three persons—Father, Son, and Holy Spirit.

The Church calls the idea of three persons in one God *the Trinity.* You won't find the word *Trinity* in the Bible; however, the idea is very much in evidence there. If you have difficulty understanding the idea of three persons in one, don't be discouraged. It is a mystery; even theologians have trouble understanding it. Any explanation we can give is inadequate, but someone has tried to make the idea more understandable by comparing the Trinity to a lighted candle. God the Father is represented by the candle itself; God the Son, by the flame; and God the Holy Spirit, by the heat generated by the candle. Three separate parts, yet the three are still one.

Another idea that may help you understand this concept can be illustrated by water. Water has three distinct forms: solid (ice), liquid (water), and vapor (steam). These are three separate substances with unique properties, and yet each is made up of a single kind of molecule. A chemist would call it H_2O. The three persons of the Trinity can be said to be different manifestations of one God.

Now let's look at some other Scriptures (Bible verses) and see what else we can learn about God.

Read **Genesis 1:1.**
2. What does this Scripture verse tell us?

_____

Yes, the second important fact we need to know about God is that He is the One who created the world in which we live and everything in it.

Read **Ephesians 1:8.**
3. What two characteristics of God are mentioned here?

_____

The third fact we need to learn about God is that He is *omniscient.*

Read **Luke 1:35** and **Romans 15:13-19.**
4. What aspect of the Holy Spirit is referred to in these verses?

_____

Read **Psalm 139:7-12.**

5. What are some of the places where the psalmist cannot escape the
    Spirit of God?

_____

In other words, the psalmist is saying that God's Spirit is everywhere.
The theological term for the fact that God is everywhere is *omnipresence*.

Read **Deuteronomy 33:27.**

6. What adjective is used to describe God in this verse?

_____

Eternal refers to the fact that God has always existed and will continue
to exist forever.

Discussion Questions: Do any of these aspects of God surprise you?
If so, which one(s)?

We don't have nearly enough space here to study all of God's
characteristics, but let's look at a few more.

7. In the space following each scripture, write down what it reveals about
    the Father:

    John 4:24 _____

    John 5:21 _____

    John 14:26_____

    1 Cor. 1:3_____

8. What characteristics of God are associated with each of the follow-
    ing scriptures?

    John 17:25_____

    1 Cor.1:9 _____

    2 Cor.1:3,4 _____

    2 Cor. 13:14_____

Of all the aspects of God's character, however, there is one which He has repeatedly tried to show His people on earth.

Read **Jeremiah 31:9.**
9. In this verse how does God describe Himself?

God sent His own Son, Jesus, to be born on earth. While here, Jesus tried to show people God's loving, father heart.

Read **John 5:17,20.**
10. What did Jesus call God in these verses?

Read **Matthew 6:9.**
11. To whom does Jesus tell us to pray?

Jesus taught that God is not only His Father, but that He wants to be our Father, too.

The Father that Jesus showed the world was not the stern, forbidding God so many believed Him to be but a God we could call "Abba," the Jewish child's equivalent to our "Daddy."

It is as a loving Father, then, that God wants us to see Him, a Father whose greatest desire is to spend eternity with us.

In the following lessons we will see the way He has provided to make this possible.

Personal Application

1. Even if I'm not ready to believe what is taught here, I will keep an open mind.
2. During the week I will restudy this chapter.
3. I will stay with this study until I complete it.

Memory Work

"God is spirit, and his worshipers must worship in spirit and in truth" *(John 4:24).*

Lesson Two

Who Needs a Savior?

Discussion Question? Is there something in your life that you would like to be rescued (saved) from right now?

Introduction

An old cartoon panel shows a street preacher speaking to a small crowd of interested spectators. "And now," he announces, "Sister Agatha is going to tell us how she was saved...from a boa constrictor."

Perhaps as implied in the cartoon you have a fuzzy idea of what Christians mean when they talk about "getting saved." Getting saved from what? If they mean getting saved from something physical (such as a boa constrictor) well, not everyone's in that kind of danger. On the other hand, if they mean getting saved from something like a nuclear war, that's another story. But you seriously doubt that that's exactly what they mean, either. So what do Christians mean when they talk about salvation, and what makes them think you need saving, anyway?

Prayer

Lord, I want to have an open mind about this whole subject of salvation. Will you please help me understand? Thank You.

Bible Study

When we talk about being saved, the primary thing we mean is being saved from the sin nature that is a part of every person born.

Perhaps the idea of having a sin nature is a hard idea for you to accept. Perhaps you think you're really not such a bad person. Oh, you have your faults, but you're not like some people. What right have Christians to say that you have a sin nature, that in fact you're a sinner?

9

We can say that everyone is born with a sin nature and is, therefore, a sinner because that's what God says about us.

Read **Genesis 8:21.**
1. What does God say about the condition of man's heart?

_____

_____

Read **Jeremiah 17:9.**
2. How is man's heart described in this verse?

_____

_____

Read **Ezekiel 11:19.**
3. How does God see man's heart?

_____

Read **Matthew 15:19.**
4. What did Jesus have to say about the human heart?

_____

_____

_____

Whew! That's a pretty bad list, isn't it? Are we trying to say that everyone is like that?

Yes, that's exactly what we're saying because that's what Jesus said.

Discussion Questions: How do you feel about Jesus' assessment of man? Do you agree or disagree? If you disagree, in what ways?

Read **Romans 1:18-32.**
These verses form one of the most accurate pictures of the world found anywhere. Let's take a look at some of the things they tell us.

5. What was the result of man's not glorifying God nor giving Him thanks (v. 21)?

_____

6. List the further, largely progressive, results of their denial of God.

V. 23 _____

V. 24 _____

V. 25 _____

V. 26 _____

V. 27 _____

V. 28 _____

Vv. 29-31 _____

_____

_____

_____

_____

V. 32 _____

_____

7. What is God's judgment on them?

_____

If we are honest, we have to admit that this description, written by the Apostle Paul almost 2,000 years ago, very well describes our world today. In less than two decades, in the name of personal freedom, we have turned our world into a cesspool that would have made past generations shudder.

Now wait a minute. Are we trying to say that everyone ever born is like that?

Read **Romans 3:23.**

8. Who does this verse say sins?

_____

Yes, *all*. The only person ever born on earth who lived a life free of sin was Jesus Christ.

Well, maybe that description fits the really "bad" people, but what about the "good" people? What about the Apostle Paul who wrote these verses? Surely, he wasn't like that.

Read **Romans 7:18,19.**

9.   How does Paul describe his own struggle against sin?

_____

_____

_____

_____

_____

Isn't that going a little too far? If even the Apostle Paul was like that, can there be hope for anyone?

You have a right to feel hopeless about the whole situation if you aren't a Christian. Maybe now you're beginning to wonder why God ever started the whole scheme in the first place. Surely, He must have known that it was going to turn out to be one big mess. Or was this whole mess His idea in the first place?

Yes, creation was God's idea and His doing. Let's see what the Bible has to say about it.

Read **Genesis 1:27.**

10.   What does this verse tell us?

_____

_____

That brings us to another question. Why did God create man in the first place?

Read **Genesis 1:28.**

11.   What was God's command to Adam and Eve?

_____

_____

Read **Genesis 3:8a.**

12.   What was God's relationship with His creation?

Because we don't have the time nor the space to go into a complete study on creation, we're going to summarize much material here in order to give you a picture of God's original intent for mankind.

God created man to have fellowship with Him and to subdue and rule the earth. Nothing wrong with that idea. Man was supposed to take charge of this planet, to be in complete control, and to be God's friend. Think what that means. Friends of the God who created the whole universe. Well, what happened between then and now? How did we ever end up in the mess we're in today?

To find the answers to those questions, we will have to wait for the next lesson.

Personal Application

1.   Can I accept the fact that everyone, including me, has done wrong—sinned?
2.   Can I accept God's verdict that I deserve death?
3.   Am I ready to have a relationship with God if someone will show me how?

Memory Work

"God blessed them and said to them, 'Be fruitful and increase in number; fill the earth and subdue it. Rule over the fish of the sea and the birds of the air and over every living creature that moves on the ground'" *(Gen. 1:28).*

What Went Wrong?

Introduction

In the last lesson we saw that man in his natural state stands condemned to death in the eyes of God, and that there is absolutely nothing in us that can help us to save ourselves. Before we learn about God's solution to this problem, we need to look back and see how the whole problem of sin began.

Prayer

Lord, these are difficult ideas to understand. I am completely dependent upon You to teach me spiritual truths. Thank You for what You will teach me today.

Review Question: Why did God create man?

Bible Study

When God created Adam and Eve, the original occupants of the earth, He made them in His own image. His command to them was to subdue and rule over all the earth. Each evening He met and talked with them. From our point of view, Adam and Eve had it made. What went wrong?

Read **Genesis 2:16,17.**
1.   What was the one restriction put on Adam and Eve?

_____

_____

2.   What would happen if they did?

Read **Genesis 3:1-7.**
3. Summarize how the serpent tempted Eve.

_____

_____

_____

4. What happened next?

_____

_____

_____

We need to take a brief detour to learn who the third character in this drama is.

Read **Revelation 20:2.**
5. What is another name for the serpent?

_____

Satan's history

Read **Ezekiel 28:11-19** and **Isaiah 14:12-15.**
The serpent in our drama was in reality Satan. The following two sections of scripture are believed by most authorities to describe his origin.

6. Who was Lucifer (Satan) (Ezek. 28:14)?

_____

7. Describe him (Ezek 28:12).

_____

_____

8. What were some of his titles (Isa. 14:12)?

_____

9. What was his condition at the time he was created (Ezek. 28:15)?

_____

10. What caused his downfall (Ezek. 28:17; Isa. 14:13,14)?

_____

_____

Read **Revelation 12:7-10.**
11. What do these verses describe?

_____

12. What was the result of that war?

_____

13. How is he described (v. 9)?

_____

Yes, Satan is the one who leads the whole world astray today as well as in the beginning. Originally created as a cherub of incredible beauty and talent, he wanted to be equal to God and succumbed to pride. A war broke out in heaven, and in the end Satan was thrown down to earth. He apparently remained on earth because it was here that he successfully tempted Adam and Eve to be disobedient to God.

Although Adam and Eve had been given rule over the entire earth, they were not satisfied. Like Satan before them, they, too, wanted to be like God.

Read **Genesis 3:8-13.**
14. What was the first result of their disobedience?

_____

These two who had fellowshipped and been friends with God were now afraid of Him. Before their disobedience, they had lived in a state of innocence knowing only good; now because of their disobedience, they knew both good and evil.

Discussion Question: What was the difference between knowing only good and knowing both good and evil?

15. Summarize their conversation with God.

_____

_____

   In their fear, they became cowardly, each refusing to accept responsibility for his part.

Discussion Questions: If they had honestly admitted their sin and responsibility, do you think God would have forgiven them and given them another chance? Why or why not?

Read **Genesis 3:14-19.**
16. Summarize the curses God put on each.

   Serpent _____

   _____

   _____

   Woman _____

   _____

   _____

   Man _____

   _____

   _____

17. What promise was given in verse 15?

   _____

   _____

Read **Genesis 3:21,24.**
18. What did God do next?

   _____

How the mighty have fallen. Because of their disobedience, Adam and Eve now had personal knowledge of evil. In a very real sense they had created an uncrossable gap between themselves and God, and they had signed their own death warrant: first spiritual death and, in time, physical death.

When they sinned, it was as though they had in a way changed the genetic structure of their human nature. Their nature, once sinless, had now become sinful and flawed. It is this nature that has been passed on to all their descendants.

If we had time to read the entire Old Testament right now, we would see the results caused by the introduction of sin into human nature and the world. We will just look at a few episodes following Adam and Eve's death.

Read **Genesis 6:5-8.**

19.   What was God's evaluation of the world by the time of Noah?

_____

_____

20.   What did God decide to do?

_____

21.   What exceptions did He make?

_____

Most of us are familiar with the story of the flood. By it God destroyed all mankind with the exception of eight people. But even in the saving of this small group of people, God had no illusions about their true nature.

Read **Genesis 8:21.**

22.   What was God's evaluation of man now?

_____

How truly God understands His creation.

Read **Genesis 11:1-9.**

23.   What do we find men trying to do a few generations later?

_____

_____

24.   What did God do?

_____

_____

We could go on and on. God continued to give men the opportunity to be obedient; again and again they failed.

Thousands of years passed, and men continued to disobey God and continued in their sins.

Was there never to be an end to the sin and failure? Was there no hope?

At one of the bleakest periods in man's history, God began to put the second part of His original plan into action.

Personal Application

1.   Am I willing to accept God's assessment of my sinful nature?
2.   Am I willing to acknowledge I can do nothing about this sinful nature?
3.   Am I ready to hear and consider His solution to the problem of sin?

Memory Work

"For all have sinned and fall short of the glory of God" (Rom. 3:23).

God's Solution—Jesus Christ

Discussion Question: If you were God, how would you resolve the sin problem?

Introduction

At the end of the last lesson, we left man in a perilous condition. Bound by his own sin, he was (and is) powerless to do anything to free himself. What can he do?

Prayer

Lord, we have come to the heart of Your salvation plan. Please burn these truths on my heart in a way that will make them easy to understand and accept. Thank You.

Bible Study

Discussion Questions: What was the most hopeless situation you were ever in? How did you escape?

All of us have been in situations we believed were hopeless. Yet, most of the time, in one way or another, we escaped. Nevertheless, no other situation, however bad, can be compared to the hopelessness man finds himself in without Jesus Christ.

Read **Romans 5:6-9** in *The Amplified Bible*.
1.   How are we described in these verses?

---

2. What did Christ do for us?

_____

3. What other names is Christ called?

_____

4. What did Christ's death for us prove?

_____

5. What did His death do?

_____

_____

Read **Romans 5:10.**
  6. What does Paul say we are before we come to God?

_____

When Adam and Eve introduced sin into the earth, in effect they and their offspring became prisoners in Satan's kingdom.

Read **Colossians 1:13.**
  7. What else did Christ's death do for us?

_____

_____

_____

Yes, God's answer to our sin problem was to send Christ to die for us. But who is this Christ? Who is this representative of God whose death accomplished so much for us?

Read **John 3:16.**
  8. Whom did God send to die for us?

_____

What a mind boggling idea! Jesus is God's Son. What kind of crazy love would cause God to send His only Son to die for people who were His enemies?

9.   What would those who believed in the Son receive?

_____

God was playing for very high stakes indeed. His creation, mankind, had disobeyed Him, turned against Him, and became His enemy. It was now actually the prisoner of His worst enemy.

To come to earth was no vacation for Jesus. In fact, it was a tremendous sacrifice on His part. Let's see why, by looking at who He was before He was born on earth.

Read **John 1:1-3.**

The Bible gives us many different names for Jesus. John, who wrote the books named after him, called Jesus "The Word," in the first verse.

10.   What do we learn about Jesus here?

_____

_____

Read **Colossians 1:15-20.**

11.   What else do we learn about Christ?

a. _____

b. _____

c. _____

d. _____

e. _____

f. _____

g. _____

h. _____

i. _____

Read **Hebrews 1:3.**

12.   What description of the Son is given here?

_____

_____

_____

Jesus the Son has always been with God the Father. He is the one who created all things and holds all things together today. Yet He gave up His position in heaven to come to earth to save us from destruction. For many years before He came, prophets told of a time in the future when He would come.

Read **Isaiah 9:6.**

13.   What are some of the descriptions of the Messiah to come?

_____

_____

Some of the prophecy was very specific and told how the Messiah might be recognized.

Read **Isaiah 7:14.**

14.   What was the sign God promised?

_____

15.   What would He be called?

_____

The prophesied birth took place many years later in Bethlehem, a town of little consequence in Israel.

Read **Matthew 1:18,20,21.**

16.   How did the angel say Jesus had been conceived?

_____

17.   What was the name Mary and Joseph were to call the baby, and what did it mean?

_____

_____

Although Jesus was the Son of God, the one who had created the whole earth, He came to earth and was born in a manger. The early years of His life were lived in obscurity. Then when He was thirty, He began His public ministry.

Read **Luke 3:21,22.**
18. What were God's words when Jesus was baptized?

_____

_____

19. What else happened?

_____

_____

Read **Luke 4:42,43.**
20. Why did Jesus say He had been sent?

_____

The good news that Jesus preached was that the kingdom of God (as opposed to the kingdom of Satan) was at hand, and that man could be reconciled to God through repentance and faith in His Son Jesus. What could be easier? Yet, most people preferred to continue in their old way of life.

In the end, Jesus died a painful death on a cross. For three days it looked as though His entire life had been in vain. Then on the third day following His death, when some of Jesus' followers went to His tomb, they found the huge stone that had sealed it rolled away, and two angels appeared.

Read **Luke 24:5-7.**
21. What had happened to Jesus?

_____

Discussion Question: Can you believe that God had the power to raise Jesus from the dead?

Read **Ephesians 1:20-22.**

22.   Where is Jesus today?

_____

23.   What is His position?

_____

_____

Read **2 Timothy 1:10.**
24.   What else did Jesus' death accomplish?

_____

_____

Read **Hebrews 7:25.**
25.   What is Jesus' doing for us today?

_____

   Jesus, like His Father, loves us so much He was willing to die to save us. Today in heaven, He is still praying that all of mankind will accept His Father's solution to the sin problem and believe in Him.
   In the next lesson, we will show you how you can accept the Father's offer.

Personal Application

   1.   Am I ready to believe that Jesus is God's Son?
   2.   Am I ready to accept God's solution to sin, Jesus Christ?
   3.   If I am having problems in believing, will I pray about it?

Memory Work

   "For God so loved the world that he gave his one and only Son, that whoever believes in him shall not perish but have eternal life" (John 3:16).

Lesson Five

Accepting Salvation

Discussion Questions: Does God's solution to the problem of sin sound too simple to you? If so, why?

Introduction

In the beginning God created a beautiful earth and human beings who had the potential to become perfect—if they would make the right choices. As we have seen, the original man and woman chose sin rather than obedience, thereby becoming flawed in their very natures. Their punishment: spiritual and physical death.

God, however, still wanted to have fellowship with His creation. But there was a problem. How could a perfect God have such fellowship when His creation was irrevocably flawed? His solution was to send His own Son to pay the penalty for man's sin and to become a spiritual Adam through whom an entire new race of men would be born.

We already know that during Jesus' lifetime, most people rejected Him and what He offered. But then as today there were those who accepted His offer of salvation. In this lesson, we shall see what we must do to obtain that salvation.

Prayer

Lord, please make Your road to salvation so crystal clear that I will fully understand the way. Thank You.

Bible Study

You will remember that in past lessons we have shown how all men need salvation and how before salvation we stand in the position of being enemies of God.

Now, we are going to learn how we can become friends of God. In many respects, the process resembles the way we are born.

Read **John 3:1-6.**
Nicodemus, a religious leader at the time of Jesus, had heard Jesus' teaching about the kingdom of God. Something about this teacher struck a chord in his heart. He wanted to learn more, but because of his position in the community, he came secretly.

1. What did Jesus tell him?

_____

The phrase *born again* is so common today it has become little more than a cliche, but we can imagine its impact on Nicodemus when he heard it for the first time.

2. What was his question?

_____

Nicodemus took Jesus' statement very literally. To his mind Jesus was talking in riddles.

3. How did Jesus explain the process of being born again?

_____

_____

In the last lesson we learned that although Jesus had a human mother, He had been conceived by the Holy Spirit. Spiritual birth comes by the Holy Spirit. What an astounding idea this must have been to Nicodemus.

Discussion Questions: Are you having trouble with the concept of spiritual rebirth? If so, what are your questions?

Read **John 3:9-12.**
4. What was Nicodemus' next question?

_____

5. How did Jesus answer?

_____

_____

_____

Spiritual truths sometimes seem so clear to Christians that they can't understand why non-Christians find them difficult, even impossible, to understand. There is a good reason for this.

Read **1 Corinthians 2:14.**
  6. Why is this so?

_____

_____

_____

Read **John 3:15-18.**
  7. What happens to the person who believes in Christ?

    V. 15 _____

    V. 16 _____

    V. 18 _____

Although different authors may describe the process differently at different times, the basic process is very simple.

Read **Acts 16:22-24.**
Paul and Silas had been thrown into jail in Philippi following a riot.

  8. Briefly summarize verses 25-28.

_____

_____

_____

_____

_____

_____

9. What was the jailer's question?

_____

10. What was Paul's answer?

_____

There are many kinds of belief, but the word *believe* in this instance is the Greek word *pisteuo*. It means to "adhere to, to cleave to, to trust, to have faith in, to rely on."

Consequently the words "Believe on the Lord Jesus Christ" really mean to have an absolute personal reliance upon the Lord Jesus Christ as Savior.

The Amplified Bible translates Paul's answer to the jailer this way: "Believe in and on the Lord Jesus Christ—that is, give yourself up to Him, take yourself out of your keeping and entrust yourself into His keeping, and you will be saved."

What else must we do?

Read **Acts 3:19.**
11. What did Peter tell his Jewish listeners?

_____

The word *repent* literally means to turn around and go in the opposite direction. As used here, it means to completely change your mind.

12. What happens when we repent?

_____

Read **Psalm 103:12.**
13. What does David say that God does with our forgiven sins?

_____

_____

Discussion Question: Can you believe that when you accept Jesus Christ as your Savior, God forgives every sin you have ever mentioned?

Read **Luke 13:3.**
14. What happens if we do not repent?

_____

Paul gives us one more essential, a step that launches our walk in a new direction.

Read **Romans 10:9,10.**

15.   What is it?

_____

The word *confess* in this case means to proclaim. Once we have taken Christ as our Lord, we need to tell someone else what we have done.

The three requirements of salvation then are

* Repentance
* Belief in Jesus Christ
* Confession to another that Jesus is Lord

Read **Acts 4:12.**

16.   Is there any other way to God?

_____

One further step is associated with salvation in the New Testament.

Read **Acts 16:33b.**

17.   What did the jailer and his family do after they were saved?

_____

We don't want to become entangled in arguments concerning the mode of baptism. To the Christian, baptism is an outward sign of an inward change. In instance after instance in the New Testament, we find new converts being baptized in water as soon as possible.

The question of whether salvation is for everyone is frequently asked. Some people feel that they have sinned too much for God to care about them. This is not what the Bible teaches.

Read **2 Peter 3:9.**

18.   How do we know that salvation is available to everyone?

_____

Personal Application

Although there may be many ideas that you do not yet understand, many new concepts for you to learn, you have been taught all you need to know in order to be saved. This is a moment of decision for you.

1. Do I believe that Jesus Christ died for my sins and was raised from the dead?
2. Am I sorry for my sins?
3. Will I ask Jesus to be my Savior right now?

If you feel you do not know how to pray, you may use this prayer: "Dear heavenly Father, I believe that Your Son Jesus died to save me and was resurrected. I am sorry for my sins; I turn my back on my old way of life, and I want to be Your child. Thank You."

If you have answered these questions and prayed, congratulations, you have just been spiritually reborn.

Right now there is great rejoicing in heaven over what you have just done.

Memory Work

"Jesus answered, 'I tell you the truth, no one can enter the kingdom of God unless he is born of water and the Spirit. Flesh gives birth to flesh, but the Spirit gives birth to spirit'" (John 3:5,6).

The Holy Spirit and His Baptism

Discussion Question: What difference did being spiritually reborn make in your life this past week?

Introduction

The history of God's activity on earth can be divided into three ages: the age of the Father—creation till the birth of Jesus, the age of Jesus—His birth through His ascension, and the age of the Holy Spirit—Pentecost and after.

Today we live in the age of the Holy Spirit. Someone has called the Holy Spirit the "Mr. X" of the Trinity. For centuries, and even for many today, He is a shadowy, ghost-like force or power emanating from the Father and the Son.

According to orthodox Christian belief, He is the third person of the Godhead or Trinity.

Prayer

Father, You have said in the Bible that spiritual truths are understood by those who are spiritual. I claim that promise for myself now, Lord. Please make these difficult truths easy for me to understand. Thank You.

Bible Study

Read **Acts 8:9-13.**
1. Summarize the events related in these verses.

_____

_____

2. After Simon was baptized and began to follow Philip, what amazed him?

_____

Read **Acts 8:14-17.**
3. Why were Peter and John sent to Samaria?

_____

_____

4. How had the Samaritan Christians been baptized?

_____

Discussion Question: If they were baptized Christians, hadn't they already received the Holy Spirit?

Because Scripture tells us that when we receive Jesus, we receive the Holy Spirit, many people are confused by this passage. The context makes us assume that it is talking about a different kind of *receiving*. Let us see if we can clear up this mystery.

Read **Acts 8:18,19.**
5. What was Simon's request of the disciples?

_____

_____

_____

Simon the sorcerer had seen many signs and great miracles taking place, but he didn't ask to receive power to perform miracles; rather, he asked to receive the authority to lay hands on people and impart the Holy Spirit to them.

Read **Acts 2:4.**
6. What is the only manifestation recorded when the disciples received the Holy Spirit?

_____

Consequently, it had to be the release of the Spirit, the speaking in tongues, which so fascinated Simon that he offered to pay for the ability to impart it to others. Poor, foolish Simon. Had his heart not been so greedy, he would have soon learned that as a Christian he had only to pray with other Christians for the Holy Spirit to manifest Himself in them.

Read **Acts 9:17** and **1 Corinthians 14:18.**
7. Who received the baptism in the Holy Spirit in this instance?

8. What does Paul say about speaking in tongues?

Read **Acts 10:44-48.**
9. What happened to the Jews listening to Peter's words?

Discussion Question: What did the Jews need to do before they could receive the baptism in the Holy Spirit?

10. What was the manifestation of the pouring out of the Spirit?

Discussion Questions: Does it bother you that the Holy Spirit was poured out on people who had not been baptized in water? If so, why?

Read **Acts 19:1-6.**
11. What were the circumstances leading up to the outpouring of the Holy Spirit in this instance?

In all these references we see the baptism in the Holy Spirit accompanied by the manifestation of speaking in tongues.

Perhaps you're wondering what is so special about speaking in tongues. When we pray in our native tongue or language, there are many handicaps. Our prayers are frequently limited by our moods, our understanding of the situation being prayed for, even our vocabulary. As we pray, we become distracted and our words stop; we find ourselves repeating the same words over and over again.

However, God has provided another way of praying—that of praying in the Spirit. When we receive our prayer language, we are being given a heavenly language with which we can pray to the Father, praise and worship Him, and intercede for others. With this new language, we bypass our intellect, our emotions, even our hang-ups.

Read **Romans 8:26,27.**

12.   What happens when we pray in the Spirit?

_____

13.   Why is He able to intercede so effectively for us?

_____

_____

When we pray in the Spirit, it is the Holy Spirit who gives us the words with which to pray. Because the Holy Spirit knows the mind of God, we can be confident that when we pray in the Spirit, we are praying according to God's will.

How do we receive the baptism in the Holy Spirit and with it our heavenly language? It is not difficult.

Reread **Acts 2:4.**

14.   If we rearrange the wording of this passage, we can see a sequence of

actions here. They were all _____

As the Spirit (enabled) them, they _____

_____ .

Those who received the baptism in the Holy Spirit that day had been praying and preparing their hearts since Jesus' return to heaven. Before we receive the infilling of the Holy Spirit, we must also prepare our hearts by confessing any known sin and asking forgiveness for it. In addition, it is very important that we renounce any involvement in cults or the occult.

Cults and the occult are sweeping the world today. TV programs feature stories about psychic phenomena and ESP. People blatantly reveal their involvement in witchcraft; evidence of satanic worship is not unusual. Children's games capitalize on the youngsters' fascination with the psychic. Movies are having a heyday with the occult and the satanic. People daily read their horoscopes in the newspapers, send for "life readings," and cultivate a morbid interest in reincarnation. Young men and women are captivated and mentally enslaved to the various cults.

What is the difference between a cult and the occult?

A cult is a false religion usually based on the beliefs and teachings of a strong leader. It proclaims a new or different way to reach God other than through faith in the atoning work of Christ on the cross. Occultism, on the other hand, is the belief in supernatural, psychic powers. Ultimately, the god of all occult groups is Satan.

In order to be free in the Spirit, we must first renounce and forsake all *"works of darkness"* (cf. 1 Corinthians 4:5 and Ephesians 5:11). If you are unwilling to do this, please do not attempt to receive the baptism in the Holy Spirit. Serious problems can result.

The second step is to ask Jesus to baptize you in the Holy Spirit. By faith, you receive His baptism. Then you release your tongue, vocal chords, and voice to the Holy Spirit. It is He who gives you the ability, but you must open your mouth and begin to speak in your heavenly language. Receiving the baptism in the Holy Spirit can be that simple.

Discussion Questions: Do you feel you are ready to receive the baptism in the Holy Spirit? If not, what is holding you back?

If you have not already received the baptism in the Holy Spirit, stop now and do these things:
1. Confess any sin you can think of in your life and ask forgiveness.
2. Renounce any involvement in a cult or the occult. If you aren't sure how to do so, you may use this prayer:
   "Father, in Jesus' name, I confess that I have sinned against You by

   _____.

   Please forgive me.
   "Satan, I hereby renounce you and all your works in my life. I command you to go in Jesus' name. By an act of my will, I close the door to you forever."
3. Choose to make Jesus the Lord of your life (see Acts 5:32).
4. Ask Jesus, the Baptizer, to baptize you now (see Mark 1:8).
5. Speak the language the Holy Spirit gives you.
6. Speak in your heavenly language every day.

Personal Application

1. List three reasons why you know that Jesus has baptized you in His Holy Spirit.
2. Find at least three scriptures which will help you handle any doubts that come up.
3. If you have not already done so, share your experience of the baptism in the Holy Spirit with another person. Write the name of

   the person you plan to share with. _____

Memory Work

"You will receive power when the Holy Spirit comes on you; and you will be my witnesses in Jerusalem, and in all Judea and Samaria, and to the ends of the earth" (Acts 1:8).

The Holy Spirit and His Work

Introduction

In a far-off kingdom many years ago, a king wanted a bride for his son, his only heir. Because the son was exemplary in every way, it was essential that the bride be worthy of her future husband.

Unfortunately, there was no one in the entire universe who met the criteria. Consequently, the father decided that he would first select a bride, then make her a fit mate for his son. Oddly enough, the bride he chose was not only a commoner, but she lived in a kingdom far away peopled by wicked citizens. The bride was very much like the people she lived among, but when she met the prince, she fell in love with him. and agreed to do what was necessary to be prepared for her future wedding.

At her promise, the king announced the engagement of his son to her, and he sent his trusted friend to groom her for the position she would one day assume.

Although anyone else would have complained about the impossibility of his errand, the friend set out confidently to accomplish the job he had been sent to do. He is still working hard at his task today.

In this parable, we can recognize many of the elements of our own relationships to God. He is the father in this story, Jesus is the son, we are the bride-to-be, and the friend is, of course, the Holy Spirit.

After we have been reconciled to the Father by accepting His Son Jesus, the Holy Spirit trains and prepares us to be a part of the Bride of Christ. He does this by sanctifying, strengthening, encouraging, and comforting us.

Prayer

Lord, You are trying to teach me such important truths. Enlarge my understanding so I may grasp what You want me to know. Thank You.

Bible Study

The word *sanctification* means both a separation *from* the world and a separation *to* God. Some versions of the Bible also use the words *consecrated* or *purified* as synonyms. In *The Amplified Bible* we frequently see the phrase "separated and set apart for pure and holy living."

Read **Luke 3:15,16.**
1. What did John the Baptist say Jesus would do?

_____

_____

The Holy Spirit is frequently symbolized by fire. Sacrifice and cleansing in the Old Testament were always associated with fire. If fire is hot enough, it will remove all impurities.

Read **1 Peter 1:2.**
2. What is one of the main purposes of our sanctification?

_____

To sanctify us, the Holy Spirit uses many different means.

3. List the means by which we are sanctified in the following verses:

John 17:17_____

Acts 26:18_____

Rom. 15:16 _____

1 Tim. 4:5_____

One of the most important purposes of sanctification is the production of spiritual fruit.

Read **Galatians 5:22,23.**
4. What is the fruit of the Spirit?

_____

_____

_____

The fruit of the Spirit is the character of Jesus. When we bear spiritual fruit, we are exhibiting His character. Reproducing Jesus' character in us is the Holy Spirit's desire for us.

Discussion Question: God sees everything as "good" in Jesus or as "worthless" in the flesh, the world, or Satan. In what ways have you not yet appropriated God's vision?

Our part in our sanctification is cooperation with the Holy Spirit. When things are revealed to us as being wrong or ungodly either through the Bible or through the Holy Spirit's personally speaking to us, it is up to us to give up or not participate in such things. The Holy Spirit will also reveal what we should be doing.

If we will read carefully, the Bible gives us many clues as to what the Holy Spirit's part in sanctification is and what our part is. When we are given phrases such as "do not offer," "get rid of," "put off," or "put on," these are what *we* are expected to do.

5. What are we told not to offer but rather to put away, put off, or lay aside in the following scriptures?

    Rom. 6:13 _____

    Eph. 4:32 _____

    Col. 3:8,9 _____

6. In the following verses we are told some of the things we are to put on or clothe ourselves with. What are they?

    Rom. 13:12 _____

    Gal. 3:27 _____

    Eph. 6:11 _____

    Col. 3:12,14 _____

    _____

Some attributes of our sinful natures cannot merely be put off. They must be put to death. However, no man can "crucify" himself. We can only be willing to have these conditions die. When we see the words "put to death," "crucify," or "mortify," the Bible is alluding to such characteristics.

Read **Colossians 3:5.**
7. What are some of the characteristics mentioned by Paul?

_____

_____

8. How are such characteristics put to death?

_____

Sanctification is a lifelong process. Our sinful natures recoil from death, but the Holy Spirit is faithful in persuading us to turn over these areas to Him in order that we will be ready for our wedding day as a fit and clean bride for our King.

Personal Question: List some of the ways the Holy Spirit is working and has worked for your sanctification.

_____

_____

Personal Question: Now list the ways you can cooperate with Him.

_____

_____

Before He died, Jesus spent many hours preparing the disciples for both His death (and resurrection) and for His return to the Father in heaven. The disciples apparently had trouble with both ideas. First, there was their refusal to accept the idea of Jesus' death; they were mentally locked into the idea of a king (Messiah) who would free Israel politically. Second, they could not accept the fact that after three years of intimate fellowship with them, Jesus was planning to go away someplace where they could not follow.

The days immediately preceding Jesus' death were ones of confusion and depression. As Jesus tried to explain the coming events to the troubled disciples, He revealed much about the Holy Spirit and the work He would do in their lives.

Insight can be gained concerning the Holy Spirit by a study of the different names He is called. For instance, in the version of the Bible we are using He is referred to as _Counselor_ as well as the _Spirit of Truth. The Amplified Bible_ calls Him _Comforter, Helper, Intercessor, Strengthener, Standby,_ and _Advocate._ (An advocate is a person who argues for your cause, a supporter or defender.) *The Amplified Bible* adds the name *Protector*.

At Pentecost the disciples received power. They also received the empowering of the Holy Spirit—the continuing and ongoing "helps" sent by the Lord.

The most familiar of these helps are called the gifts of the Spirit.

Read **1 Corinthians 12:7-11.**
9. List the gifts of the Spirit.

_____

_____

_____

_____

10. How are the gifts distributed?

_____

Read **1 Corinthians 14:1.**
11. What is to be our attitude toward the spiritual gifts?

_____

Read **1 Corinthians 14:12-17.**
12. What is one of the prime reasons to seek spiritual gifts?

_____

Paul's list of the gifts of the Holy Spirit cannot be understood as a total list of the gifts or helps given the Spirit-filled Christian. The Bible and individual Christian's lives are filled with examples of the Spirit's help, both spiritual and temporal, in times of need. Whatever the real need of the Christian, the Holy Spirit is there to meet and provide for it.

13. Write the kind of help given by the Holy Spirit in the following references:

Isa. 63:14 _____

Acts 9:31 _____

Rom. 5:5 _____

Rom. 8:2 _____

Rom. 8:11 _____

Rom. 8:26 _____

Rom. 14:17 _____

Rom. 15:13 _____

Eph. 3:16 _____

2 Tim. 1:7 _____

Read **John 16:13.**
14.   What else does Jesus say the Holy Spirit will do?

_____

Read **John 8:32.**
15.   What will the truth do for us?

_____

    Although many talk of freedom, the Christian is the only truly free person in the world today.
    When Jesus returned to the Father, He did not leave us as orphans or comfortless. By the presence of the Holy Spirit within us, we have all the power and help we need to live victorious Christian lives and to stand firm through all conditions and situations of our lives.

Personal Application

1.   Write a paragraph summarizing your understanding of the Holy Spirit as being the spirit of Jesus.
2.   List the different kinds of help available to you through the Holy Spirit.
3.   Which areas in your life do you need to give the Holy Spirit permission to work in right now?

Memory Work

    "When the Counselor comes, whom I will send to you from the Father, the Spirit of truth who goes out from the Father, he will testify about me. And you also must testify, for you have been with me from the beginning" (*John 15:26,27*).

The Bible

Introduction

All religions have a set of beliefs by which they are guided. The Christian beliefs are set forth in a book called *The Bible*. Actually, the Greek word *biblia* from which we get our word *Bible* means "books."

Our Christian Bible is made up of sixty-six books in all: thirty-nine in the Old Testament and twenty-seven in the New. The word *testament* means "covenant." It refers to the covenants God has made with His people, first the Jews, then those who would follow the teachings of Jesus Christ.

Known by many names, *Scripture* or *the Scriptures, the Word, the Law,* to name a few, the Bible constitutes the ultimate authority on matters of faith and practice for Christians.

Prayer

Lord, teach me how to understand this Book You have given to us to be our "rule of faith and practice." Thank You.

Bible Study

How did the Bible come into existence? What is its purpose? What does it contain? To answer these questions, we must see what the Bible has to say about itself.

Read **2 Timothy 3:16,17.**
1. Where did Scripture (the Bible) come from?

_____

Discussion Question: What does the expression *God-breathed* mean?

God-breathed means that the writers of the Bible were men whom God inspired or shared His mind and will with so that they in turn could share them with many others. Although God used ordinary men to write the Bible, He is the real author. This fact alone makes the Bible different from any other book. Because it is made up of the intentions or purposes of God, Christians do not have the right to pick and choose which parts of the Bible they will believe. The Bible as originally written must be believed in its entirety.

2.   What are some of the ways the Bible may be used?

_____

_____

Read **John 6:63.**
A large section of the New Testament is made up of the words spoken by Jesus Christ when He lived on earth.

3.   What does Jesus say about His words?

_____

_____

Read **Hebrews 4:12.**
4.   What does this verse tell us the Word of God is?

_____

_____

God is not using poetic language in this verse. He is telling us that His Word is actually alive spiritually.

5.   What does it do?

_____

_____

_____

Let's think about this statement a minute. In it, God is saying that His words are so powerful they will actually enable us to judge our own thoughts and attitudes—to determine whether or not they are godly.

Read **John 8:31,32.**

6. What will happen if we hold to (believe and obey) Jesus' teachings?

_____

The entire history of mankind is a history of man's bondage and captivity. Created to be free, man immediately sold himself into slavery to Satan. Although God has rescued and freed him time and time again, man has soon returned to his slavery. In these two verses, Jesus reveals the gateway to eternal freedom.

7. Before we go on, let's summarize the particular characteristics and abilities of God's Word we have looked at so far.

What it is   **What it can do**

_____   _____

_____   _____

_____   _____

_____   _____

_____   _____

No other book would dare to make such claims about itself because no other book can even approach the abilities of the Word of God. God has put life and power into His words. Let's look at some of the power contained in them.

Read **Psalm 107:20.**

8. What is accomplished by God's Word in this verse?

_____

Scripture, properly understood, never contradicts itself. What we read of God's Word doing in this Old Testament verse, we see Jesus, God's living Word, doing in the flesh.

Read **Luke 7:1-10.**

9. This is the story of the Roman centurion whom Jesus commended for his faith. When Jesus offered to come to the centurion's home

to heal the man's servant, what was the centurion's statement of faith (v. 7)?

_____

10. What happened?

_____

The power of God's Word to heal was demonstrated time and time again during Jesus' lifetime and afterwards by His followers.

Read **Romans 10:17.**
11. What else can we receive through the Word of God?

_____

There are times when we all lack sufficient faith. One of the best ways for gaining faith is through hearing or reading God's Word.
In Psalm 119, we find the psalmist giving credit to God's Word for many different abilities.

12. List what it does in each case.

V. 1 _____

V. 9 _____

V. 11 _____

V. 24 _____

V. 25 _____

V. 28 _____

V. 29 _____

V. 32 _____

V. 35 _____

V. 41 _____

V. 49 _____

V. 52 _____

V. 98 _____

V. 99 _____

V. 104 _____

V. 165 _____

The Bible is many books—the history of God's working among His people, poetry, law, prophesy. Perhaps as important as anything else, it gives us a map that shows us the way God wants us to walk during our lives.

Read **Matthew 22:37-39.**
13. What did Jesus say were the two most important commandments?

_____

_____

_____

Read **Matthew 6:31-33.**
14. What are we to seek first?

_____

15. If we do so, what further reward will we receive?

_____

Read **Psalm 34:12-14.**
16. What are we to turn from?

_____

17. What are we to do?

_____

Read **John 17:3.**
18. How does Jesus describe eternal life?

_____

In these few pages, we have tried to give you a small sampling of what the Bible is and what it holds. The Bible is a treasure chest for anyone who will read it, believe it, and practice it. In its pages are found the keys to salvation, the spiritual walk, and life eternal. It is a study that will take a lifetime.

Personal Application

1. Will I allow the Bible to be my final authority on all matters of faith and practice?
2. Will I set time aside each day to read and study the Bible?
3. If possible, will I join a good Bible study to learn more about the Bible?

Memory Work

"The word of God is living and active. Sharper than any double-edged sword, it penetrates even to dividing soul and spirit, joints and marrow; it judges the thoughts and attitudes of the heart" (Heb. 4:12).

Walking Closely with the Lord

Introduction

Of the great number of people who accept Jesus as their Savior each year, a large percentage of them go no further or else they "drop out" within a short time. One of the major reasons why is because they don't avail themselves of the "helps" provided by the Lord.

Although a whole study could be written on each of the following topics, we have space only to briefly consider each of them.

Prayer

Dearest Father, now that I have found You, I want to learn how to walk closer and closer to you. Please stimulate my intelligence so that I can understand the many things You have to teach me in this lesson. Thank You.

Bible Study

Discussion Questions: What is the most significant difference you have noticed about yourself since you have accepted Jesus Christ and been baptized in the Holy Spirit? Has anyone noticed a difference in you?

Confession of Sins
At the time of your conversion, all your past sins were forgiven, erased, Because Jesus had paid the penalty for them by dying on the cross, God saw you as someone who had never sinned. But what happened the next time you sinned.

Read **1 John 1:8-10.**
God has no illusions about His creation.
1. What happens if we claim to be without sin?

50

_____

_____

_____

God knows that as long as we live in this world, no matter how hard we try, sooner or later, we will sin. However, He has made provision for any present or future sins we may commit.

2. What is that provision (v. 9)?

_____

3. What happens when we do this?

_____

Read **1 John 2:1,2.**
4. Why does God do this (v. 2)?

_____

Yes, if we will confess our sins, God is willing to forgive us each time because Jesus has already paid the penalty for those sins.

5. What does Jesus do for us today?

_____

Discussion Question: Against what or whom is he defending us?

Read **Hebrews 7:24,25.**
6. What does this verse tell us Jesus does?

_____

If you have ever wondered what Jesus is doing today, this verse tells us that He is continuing His efforts on our behalf. His death on the cross paid the penalty for our sins; His intercession (along with our confession) keeps our records clear of sin so that we can one day appear before the Father, spotless and holy.

We cannot emphasize strongly enough the necessity of availing ourselves of this method of remaining "clean" in God's eyes. When we don't recognize our own sins, John points out that we deceive ourselves—we open the door to deception of many kinds and to the deceiver himself, Satan.

Prayer
Read **Matthew 14:23; Mark 1:35; Luke 6:12.**
7.   What do we find Jesus doing in these verses?

_____

We find Jesus praying before all important events of His life,

8.   Tell what happened after Jesus prayed in each instance.

Luke 6:13 _____

Luke 9:28-36 _____

_____

Luke 11:1,2 _____

_____

Luke 22:39-54 _____

If Jesus, who was without sin, would not even try to live without daily prayer, why do we, His followers, think we can? A fairly recent survey reveals that the average born-again Christian devotes only a few minutes a day to prayer.

Dear Christians, Christianity alone of all religions has a God who takes a vital interest in us and urges us to have daily conversation with Him. Jesus continues to pray for us in heaven. Can we do less?

Read **Psalm 25:14.**
9.   What will God do for those who fear him?

_____

The usual way God confides in us is when we are praying.

God wants to fellowship with His people. One of the most important avenues He has made available for this fellowship is through prayer.

Communion
Before He died, Jesus demonstrated still another way we could com-

municate with God. This is through what we commonly call The Lord's Supper or Holy Communion.

Read **Luke 22:7-20.**

10.   What Jewish holiday was being celebrated?

_____

11.   What two kinds of food did Jesus use?

_____

Many of us have designated special meanings to the foods that Jesus used in this first communion service. But Jesus selected ordinary food that would be served at any Jewish meal—bread and wine.

Bread was the staple commodity of most Jewish meals. A flat, unleavened bread, it was nutritious enough to satisfy most of the dietary needs of the people. Because much of the water of that area was contaminated, it was common practice for the people there to disinfect it by mixing one-third wine with it.

12.   When did Jesus take the bread?

_____

While we make our communion a ritual apart from a regular meal, this original communion service was part of the meal Jesus was eating with His disciples.

13.   What did Jesus say the bread represented?

_____

14.   When did He take the wine?

_____

15.   What did He call the wine?

_____

16.   What was Jesus' blood poured out for?

_____

17.   What did Jesus tell the disciples to do (v. 19b)?

_____

Paul gives us some further information concerning the Lord's Supper.

Read **1 Corinthians 11:23-32.**
18.   What does Paul say happens to a person who takes communion in an unworthy manner?

_____

_____

19.   What should we do before we take communion?

_____

Discussion Question: How can we examine ourselves?

We examine ourselves to see if we have any unconfessed sin in our lives. Should we become aware of any, we confess it to the Lord and ask His forgiveness. Then we are ready to share this holy meal with both the Lord and with our fellow Christians.

The fourth tool the Lord has given us for our straight and narrow (exact) walk is fellowship with other Christians. We will discuss this in the next lesson.

Personal Application

1.   Which "tools" am I presently not using?
2.   Will I start using them immediately?
3.   Will I give top priority to them until they are established habits in my life?

Memory Work

"If we claim to be without sin, we deceive ourselves and the truth is not in us. If we confess our sins, he is faithful and just and will forgive us our sins and purify us from all unrighteousness" (1 John 1:8-10).

Lesson Ten

The Body of Christ

Introduction

When we speak of the Body of Christ or the Church, as it is more commonly called today, we are not speaking of any particular denomination or individual group of believers. Rather, we mean those believers in all denominations from every area and race of the world who profess Christ as their Savior and Lord.

Prayer

Lord, You have so many things to teach me. Make this lesson crystal clear in my mind. Thank You.

Bible Study

The Christian Church was born on Pentecost when the Holy Spirit was given to the followers of Jesus.

Read **Acts 2:1-5.**
1. Briefly summarize the coming of the Holy Spirit to the believers.

_____

_____

Read **Acts 2:6-13.**
2. What was the reaction of those in the city?

_____

_____

_____

Read **Acts 2:17-41.**
   3.   What did Peter do?

_____

   4.   What was the response of the crowd (v. 37)?

_____

   5.   What was Peter's response?

_____

_____

   6.   How many were baptized that day?

_____

Discussion Question: Why do you think God chose that particular day for the beginning of the Church?

Read **Acts 2:42.**
   7.   To what did these new converts devote themselves?

_____

_____

   This is the simple account of the beginning of the Christian Church. The Bible tells us that "the Lord added to their number daily those who were being saved."

Read **Acts 2:43.**
   8.   What characterized the Early Church?

_____

Read **Acts 8:1.**
   9.   How did the Church spread to Judea and Samaria?

_____

Through persecution and evangelism, the followers of Jesus became His witnesses in Jerusalem, in Judea, in Samaria, and to the ends of the earth just as Jesus had prophesied. Everywhere Christians went, they took along with them their living, vibrant faith, and the Church grew until it encompassed the entire world.

The Bible teaches us that the Christian life cannot be lived in a vacuum. As planned by Jesus, it should be lived in the company and close fellowship of other Christians.

Read **1 Corinthians 12:12-27.**

10. To what does Paul compare Christians?

_____

11. What is the individual Christian?

_____

In this wonderful section on the Body of Christ, Paul explains our relationship to one another.

12. What three conclusions do we come to from this section?

V. 20 _____

V. 21,22 _____

V. 25 _____

Read **1 Corinthians 12:4-11.**

13. For what are the manifestations of the Spirit given (v. 7)?

_____

Read **Ephesians 4:11-14.**

14. Why did Christ create the different positions in the Church?

_____

15. For what purpose?

_____

16. Until what happens?

_____

Read **Ephesians 4:15,16.**

17. Who is our Head?

_____

18. What do we achieve from Him?

_____

_____

19. How is this accomplished?

_____

The Early Church seems to have understood this concept of fellowship better than we do.

Read **Acts 2:42-47** and **Acts 4:23-25.**

20. What things did the early believers do that expressed their unity and fellowship?

_____

_____

_____

_____

It is not always easy to live together with other Christians in love and harmony, but in his letter to the Romans, Paul gives us some very helpful tips.

Read **Romans 14.**

21. Summarize Paul's main points.

_____

_____

_____

_____

Read **Romans 15:1-13.**

22.   Summarize his main ideas in these verses.

_____

_____

_____

_____

_____

Personal Application

1.   Do I see all sincere Christians as part of the Body of Christ, or am I guilty of believing that members of my own group are "special"?
2.   Am I doing anything in my local body or in the body as a whole to break the unity of the Church?
3.   Am I willing to forego all judgment on disputable matters?
4.   Will I sincerely try to "build up" the other members of the Body?

Memory Work

   "Now you are the body of Christ, and each one of you is a part of it" (1 Cor. 12:27).

Lesson Eleven

The Return of Jesus

Introduction

A Spirit-filled life on earth is only the beginning for the Christian. Throughout Jesus' ministry here, he spoke of future events—increasingly hard times for the earth and its people and a glorious future with Him for Christians.

Prayer

Lord, I thank You for everything You have taught me through this study and what You will teach me today about my eternal life with You. Thank You.

Bible Study

Read **Matthew 24:1-8.**
1. What question did the disciples ask Jesus?

    _____

2. What major events or catastrophes did Jesus name?

    _____

    _____

    _____

Discussion Question: Which of these signs prophesied by Jesus have already taken place or are taking place today? Be specific.

60

3. How did Jesus describe them?

_____

Read **Matthew 24:9-13.**
4. What further ominous signs did Jesus mention?

_____

_____

_____

_____

_____

_____

_____

Discussion Question: How many of these events have either taken place or are taking place today?

Read **Matthew 24:23-29.**
5. What powers will the false Christs and prophets have?

_____

6. What further signs of the end did Jesus give (v. 29)?

_____

_____

Read **2 Thessalonians 2:1-8.**
7. What must happen before Jesus returns?

_____

8. What will happen to him?

_____

_____

Read **Matthew 24:14,30,31.**
9. What else must happen?

_____

_____

10. What will happen then?

_____

The earth on which we live has only a temporary existence.

11. How will the Son of Man (Christ) come?

_____

Read **Acts 1:10,11.**

Discussion Question: What protection does Jesus give the Christian against being deceived?

The Christian who knows his Bible and the Lord does not have to worry about being deceived. Jesus very specifically describes His return.

Read **Matthew 24:36.**
12. Why should Christians not try to predict the exact time of Jesus' return?

_____

_____

Read **2 Peter 3:8-10.**
13. What is one reason for Jesus' delay?

_____

14. What is the final destiny of the earth and heavens we know?

_____

_____

_____

Read **Matthew 25:31-33,46.**
15.   What is the ultimate destiny of the wicked?

_____

We now want to take a look at the eternal destiny that awaits those who believe in Jesus Christ.
Before His death Jesus told His disciples about His death, resurrection, and return to heaven.

Read **John 16:6,7.**
16.   What was one reason for Jesus' return to heaven?

_____

Read **John 14:1-3.**
17.   What did Jesus promise His disciples?

_____

_____

Read **1 Thessalonians 4:13-18.**
18.   What will happen to those Christians who have already died?

_____

19.   What about those who are still alive?

_____

_____

20.   What will happen to us?

_____

Before that great day, however, the Lord has warned us that many of us may have to suffer persecution for our faith in Him.

Read **Mark 13:11.**
21.   What should we not do if we are arrested?

_____

22. Why?

_____

Read **Matthew 24:42-44.**
23. What is Jesus' advice to us during these times?

_____

Read **1 Thessalonians 5:1-11.**
24. What advice does Paul add to this?

_____

_____

_____

Read **Matthew 24:13.**
25. What good news did Jesus reveal?

_____

Read **1 Corinthians 2:9.**
26. How does Paul describe our inheritance?

_____

_____

Read **1 Peter 1:4.**
27. How does Peter describe our inheritance?

_____

Personal Application

1. What am I doing to further the spreading of the Gospel to the whole world?
2. What am I doing to ensure my faithfulness to the Lord?
3. Am I ready to suffer persecution for the Lord's sake?

Memory Work

"No eye has seen, no ear has heard, no mind has conceived what God has prepared for those who love him" (1 Cor. 2:9).